HIDDEN PLACES AROUND
ROCHESTER
NEW YORK

Your guide to experiencing 50 unique destinations in Rochester, the Finger Lakes, and Western New York.

Debi Bower

gevany
PUBLISHING

Gevany Publishing, PO Box 213, Rush, NY 14543

ISBN: 979-8-9874620-6-5

Library of Congress Control Number: 2025913439

Visit the author's website at daytrippingroc.com.

Edited by Michele Elder.

Photography by Debi Bower. Front cover: Rock City Park, Our Lady of Fatima Shrine, Sycamore Hill Gardens, The Eternal Flame. Back cover: The Hidden Sidewalk, Corbett's Glen, Chimney Bluffs.

50 Hidden Places Around Rochester, New York

CONCEALED PATHWAYS

STORIED EARTHWORKS

18. The Eternal Flame Trail

19. Grimes Glen

20. Holley Canal Falls

21. Stony Brook

22. Akron Falls

23. Rock City Park

24. Medina Falls

25. Fillmore Glen

26. Moss Lake Preserve

27. Hemlock Lake Park

DESIGNED LANDSCAPES

28. Lamberton Conservatory

29. The Sunken Garden

30. Durand Eastman Park Arboretum

31. Griffis Sculpture Park

32. Webster Arboretum

33. Delaware Park Japanese Garden

34. Sycamore Hill Gardens

35. Ellwanger Garden

36. Linwood Gardens

Introduction

Not every remarkable place around Rochester and Western New York appears in tourism brochures. Some hide behind historic homes, along quiet trails, or in plain sight. Others are state parks or sacred spaces beloved by locals but often overlooked by visitors. What they share is a sense of mystery and reward—a chance to slow down and connect more deeply with your surroundings.

This guide features 50 such places. Each chapter includes a brief description and an insider tip to help you gain a deeper understanding of the topic. Some are perfect for a short detour, while others can anchor an afternoon or weekend outing. Expect varied terrain from smooth to rugged.

Treat these places with care—stay on trails and take only memories. Whether you're seeking solitude or a fresh perspective, let this guide inspire you to explore differently and uncover the quiet magic just beyond the beaten path.

The Hidden Sidewalk

Beach Avenue, Rochester

Rochester's Hidden Sidewalk is a barely marked public pathway that slips between the backyards of elegant Beach Avenue homes and the edge of Lake Ontario. This slender concrete strip hugs the shoreline, offering one of the city's most peaceful, unobstructed lake views. Look carefully for narrow openings opposite Cloverdale and Clematis Streets.

Once you're on the walk, spur paths appear every few houses, linking back to Beach Avenue. Stay on the sidewalk itself—lawns and patios are private property. Take this short 0.4-mile walk slowly to enjoy the steady wash of waves and the vast horizon that create a feeling of escape.

INSIDER TIP: Park near Abbott's Frozen Custard, grab a treat, and stroll west along Beach Avenue until you spot an entrance. Turn around at the end and retrace your steps for a different perspective.

The Autism Nature Trail

Letchworth State Park, 6773 Trailside Road, Castile

Just inside Letchworth State Park's Castile entrance, the Autism Nature Trail (ANT) offers a one-mile, ADA-accessible loop intentionally designed for neurodiverse visitors, but is welcome to anyone seeking a more gentle, self-paced outdoor experience. Shaded and thoughtfully planned, the trail features eight themed activity stations, each inviting you to engage with nature on your terms, including the Music Circle, where oversized instruments invite rhythmic play.

The trail's wide, stable surface winds through the forest trees and meadows blooming with wildflowers. Clear icons on signage help visitors of all abilities understand and choose their experiences. It's peaceful, accessible, and genuinely welcoming—a rare corner of a dramatic park that has been intentionally made calm.

INSIDER TIP: Visit midweek or early in the morning for the quietest experience, then stop by the nearby Humphrey Nature Center for interactive exhibits, family programs, and seasonal nature walks.

The Jump-Off Overlook

Ontario County Park, 6475 Gannett Hill Park Drive, Naples

Perched at an elevation of over 2,200 feet, the Jump-Off Overlook in Naples delivers a panoramic sweep of the Bristol Hills without the need for a strenuous hike. From the parking area atop Gannett Hill, a short gravel path leads through a stand of pines to a wooden platform where the land drops away in a dramatic cliff. From there, you can enjoy a stunning view of CR-33/West Hollow Road and the backside of Bristol Mountain. Whether you linger for 10 minutes or an hour, the quiet and the scale invite deep breaths and stillness.

The trail itself is just a small part of a vast network of footpaths known as the Finger Lakes Trail. This section is a part of the Bristol Hills Branch Trail in the Western Finger Lakes Region.

INSIDER TIP: Visit in mid to late October for a breathtaking view during peak foliage season. It's a perfect stop along a scenic drive toward Naples.

Corbett's Glen

415 Penfield Road, Brighton

Nestled between an expressway and two highly trafficked roads near the Penfield–Brighton border, Corbett's Glen is a glorious green space in a suburban jungle. To visit Corbett's Glen North, start from the parking lot on Penfield Road. You can follow stone dust, wood chip, and pine needle trails toward the south end. The pathways are easy to navigate, although some parts of the trail, such as the Stone Steps, can be steep.

Alternatively, a short walk from the Glen Road entrance drops you into a shady gorge where Allen Creek flows through a picturesque tunnel, forming three waterfalls beneath a lush tree canopy. The trails here lead through marsh meadows, shrublands, and wetlands.

INSIDER TIP: Visitors entering by Glen Road should park at the top of the road and walk through the tunnel to reach the trail. However, for those with valid permits, two designated accessible parking spaces are located just beyond the tunnel.

Turning Point Park Boardwalk

260 Boxart Street, Rochester

Turning Point Park's most striking feature is a 3,572-foot-long bridge over the Genesee River turning basin in Rochester. The boardwalk guides visitors directly over the water, where they can observe blue herons, swans, turtles, deer, and other wildlife. For a minimal elevation change, consider starting your walk from the north at Petten Street, near the marina and O'Rorke Bridge. Along this section, you'll encounter the abandoned 150-foot boat, the Spirit of Rochester.

To start at the south end, park in the Boxart Street lot. Most people walk north down the steep, paved road toward the river, but you can also take the train-grade path by heading south for a half mile from the parking lot and turning left at the fork near Brewster Harding Park. Enhance your experience by exploring beyond the boardwalk. The entire Genesee Riverway Trail spans 12 miles, extending from Lake Ontario to Genesee Valley Park.

INSIDER TIP: The route through Bullock's Woods follows a seasonal creek, where you can hear a small waterfall just off the path after heavy rains.

Channing H. Philbrick Park

1 Linear Park Drive, Penfield

Irondequoit Creek drops 90 feet over a one-mile stretch through this Penfield town park, creating the cascades that make it a unique experience. While the Irondequoit Creek Trail spans the park's length and beyond, the most exciting section lies east of Linear Park Drive. Near the kiosk next to the upper parking lot, find the easy-to-walk dirt path that follows the creek toward a 500-foot-long footbridge.

The trails on the east side of the park include the Honey Creek Trail and Mills Trail, with the Fishing Trail on the west side. Continue exploring Irondequoit Creek by following it south to Spring Lake Park or north to Panorama Valley Park.

INSIDER TIP: While walking on the Irondequoit Creek Trail between Linear Park Drive and the footbridges, keep an eye out for a small, unmarked trail that leads up to Honey Creek's waterfall, where it tumbles into the ravine to join Irondequoit Creek.

Helmer Nature Center

154 Pinegrove Avenue, Irondequoit

Established in 1973 and named for former superintendent Earle Helmer, the center functions as a 45-acre "outdoor classroom" woven into West Irondequoit's science curriculum and open to the public year-round. Follow one and a half miles of dirt, wood chip, boardwalk, and gravel paths, where tree roots cross the valley floor. The rolling, densely wooded landscape makes Helmer ideal for woodland discovery.

Gently descending paths draw you into the valley, where the steep surrounding slopes muffle suburban sights and sounds, fostering a tranquil atmosphere. Continue to an observation deck beside a bog that serves as a prime spot for viewing bullfrogs and water striders. Enjoy the nature center year-round by using snowshoes and skis to cross snow-blanketed fields. On most Saturdays in January and February, visitors can rent snowshoes once the snowpack reaches a depth of six to eight inches.

INSIDER TIP: Visit in March for maple-sugaring activities, including tapping demonstrations, tastings, and hikes that celebrate the harvest.

Washington Grove

Cobbs Hill Park, 1 Nunda Boulevard, Rochester

Washington Grove is a 26-acre old-growth forest nestled next to Rochester's Cobbs Hill Reservoir—a quiet, natural space that feels surprisingly remote for an urban park. A glorious canopy of towering maple, cherry, sassafras, and tulip poplar trees offers a shaded respite from the summer heat. Part of the Pinnacle Range, trails weave through glacial kettles, mossy logs, and scattered boulders, leading to two ever-changing, graffiti-tagged water towers. There are several trailheads around the forest, including one at the end of Nunda Boulevard and two along the treeline by the reservoir.

Volunteers with the Friends of Washington Grove work to remove invasive plants and protect newly planted trees. Stay on visible trails to avoid damaging sensitive areas.

INSIDER TIP: For the most direct access, enter Washington Grove via the Nunda Boulevard trailhead.

Keuka Outlet Trail

Penn Yan/Dresden

The seven-mile Keuka Outlet Trail links Keuka Lake to Seneca Lake. Once a canal and later a rail line, the corridor is now a tree-shaded path where waterfalls, ruins, and birdsong replace the clatter of industry.

In the village of Penn Yan, a 1.3-mile paved section allows for a stroll along the outlet to bakeries, cafes, restaurants, and Penn Yan's picturesque Main Street. Leaving the village, the multiuse dirt, gravel, and crushed-stone trail follows the former Fall Brook Railroad track bed, offering a variety of recreational activities, including hiking, biking, and horseback riding. Notable highlights include Seneca Mills Falls and Cascade Mills Falls, both of which have nearby parking areas, providing easy access and a short, flat walk.

INSIDER TIP: After your adventure, treat yourself to ice cream from Seneca Farms or Spotted Duck, two beloved local spots just a short drive away.

Meridian Centre Park

680 Westfall Road, Brighton

Hidden behind the Jewish Home campus in Brighton and beyond the athletic fields, there is a hidden oasis nestled between the Erie Canal and I-590.

A flat, 1.5-mile loop of packed gravel and wood chip paths—ideal for jogging, strolling with young children, or brisk walks with a leashed dog—and a boardwalk with picturesque wooden arches wind through arboretum plantings, open fields, and a cattail marsh buzzing with songbirds. Benches and a small overlook provide a peaceful spot for reflection and birdwatching.

INSIDER TIP: Park in the lot behind 100 Meridian Centre Drive, next to the playground. From the main loop, take one of the short connector trails up the embankment to the Erie Canalway Trail; turn left (west) toward South Winton Road to return to the lot. This adds about one half mile and a gentle 30-foot climb, perfect if you want to extend the outing without retracing your steps.

Oatka Creek Park

9797 Union Street, Wheatland

Oatka Creek Park in Wheatland is Monroe County's third-largest park—461 acres of undeveloped land and a rippling brown trout stream. A network of wide, color-blazed trails loops through tall grasslands and into hardwood forests. The mown-grass meadow trails are perfect for observing wildflowers along with the birds and insects that flourish among them. Follow the purple trail to a bridge spanning Oatka Creek.

What sets Oatka apart is the sense of spacious calm. Because the land was once farmland, sightlines remain broad; you can observe the park's wildlife from a safe distance. Some paths may be muddy or shared with horses, but there is little elevation change.

INSIDER TIP: Oatka Creek Park is particularly scenic in late summer when vibrant wildflower meadows frame a grove of white quaking aspen trees along the Black Trail.

Iroquois National Wildlife Refuge

1101 Casey Road, Basom

The Iroquois National Wildlife Refuge, spanning 10,800 acres of wetlands, forests, and grasslands, is situated midway between Rochester and Buffalo in the town of Basom. Together with the Oak Orchard and Tonawanda Wildlife Management Areas—often called the Alabama Swamp Complex—it forms one of Western New York's richest wildlife landscapes.

Short, level footpaths and dike roads lead to cattail marshes where tundra swans and sandhill cranes rest. Observation platforms and boardwalk loops, such as Swallow Hollow and Kanyoo, enable visitors to observe bald eagles, herons, and numerous songbirds without disturbing the fragile habitat. With no entrance fee, few crowds, and horizons free of development, the refuge feels gloriously remote. It's as much a place for quiet as for rare species—an invitation to slow down and move at marsh speed.

INSIDER TIP: Plan your visit to coincide with the spring migrations, beginning in March. May is the peak month for observing shorebirds and warblers.

Green Lakes

7900 Green Lakes Road, Fayetteville

Green Lake and Round Lake, located within Green Lakes State Park just east of Syracuse in Fayetteville, are among the most stunning bodies of water in New York. These rare meromictic lakes, where surface and deep waters don't mix, shimmer in blue-green hues that seem almost tropical. Their unusual clarity and coloration make them one of the region's most captivating natural wonders.

A three-mile trail circles the lakes, hugging the shoreline and offering scenic views from nearly every bend. Interpretive signs explain the lakes' unique geology, including microbial mats and the scientific significance of their undisturbed depths. Round Lake, protected as a National Natural Landmark, is bordered by old-growth forest, including the Tuliptree Cathedral, renowned for its towering tulip poplars.

INSIDER TIP: Due to the sensitive nature of the lakes, no outside floating vessels are allowed. However, rowboat and kayak rentals are available at the boathouse, including clear-bottom tandem kayaks, to explore Green Lake.

Chimney Bluffs

7700 Garner Road, Wolcott

Chimney Bluffs State Park in Huron showcases one of the most dramatic natural landscapes in New York. Centuries of wind, rain, and waves have eroded a glacial drumlin into a jagged ridgeline of pinnacles and spires that tower nearly 150 feet above Lake Ontario.

The Bluff Trail winds along the top of the cliffs, offering breathtaking views but also presenting challenges. Due to erosion and safety concerns, portions of the trail may be temporarily closed or off-limits. Visitors are strongly advised against descending or climbing the bluff faces. The soil is unstable, and the formations are both fragile and potentially dangerous. Fortunately, the shoreline on the park's eastern side provides lake-level views of the towering formations. The view from a kayak is truly unforgettable.

INSIDER TIP: Skip the state park fee by starting at the free lot on East Bay Road. From there, walk the shoreline westward for close-up views—especially beautiful in late-afternoon light when the sun peaks between the spires.

The Genesee River Gorge

Rochester

Rochester's Genesee River gorge offers some of the most dramatic scenery in the city, with High Falls, Middle Falls, and Lower Falls showcasing the river's 200-foot drop through Rochester's urban corridor. High Falls, a 96-foot cascade located in the heart of downtown, is poised to become the centerpiece of the future High Falls State Park.

Further north, Maplewood Park offers a quieter experience. Designed by Frederick Law Olmsted, the park features walking paths, scenic overlooks, and a formal rose garden that blooms from June to November. A short walk under the Driving Park Bridge leads to the 110-foot Lower Falls and the 25-foot Middle Falls, now part of an RG&E hydroelectric dam. Connecting Maplewood and Seneca Parks, the Pure Waters Pedestrian Bridge offers a river crossing with expansive views of the gorge.

INSIDER TIP: From Lower Falls Park, you can walk south to Middle Falls via the Genesee Riverway Trail. The bridge over the RG&E dam offers excellent views, but access is occasionally restricted when the utility closes it for maintenance or safety reasons.

The Niagara River Gorge

Niagara Falls

Downstream from Niagara Falls State Park, the Niagara River Gorge offers a raw, rugged contrast to the polished attractions above. Carved over thousands of years as the falls receded upstream, this dramatic chasm reveals sheer canyon walls, thunderous rapids, and ancient rock layers.

Trails wind through Devil's Hole and Whirlpool State Parks, ranging from strenuous descents to scenic rim walks. Highlights along the way include the thigh-burning Whirlpool Rapids Trail that hugs Class V whitewater, the family-friendly Great Gorge Railway Trail tracing an 1890s trolley bed between the Discovery Center and Whirlpool Rapids Bridge, and Giant Rock—an immense monolith reached from the Devil's Hole staircase that delivers head-on views of the emerald Whirlpool below. The Niagara Gorge Rim Trail offers wide, flat paths with panoramic cliffside vistas.

INSIDER TIP: Take the Schoellkopf Power Station Elevator from the Niagara Gorge Discovery Center for easy access to the river's edge—ideal for those who want to experience being down in the gorge without the steep climb.

Havana Glen

135 Havana Glen Road, Montour Falls

Just south of Watkins Glen, Havana Glen Park in Montour Falls offers a quieter, more intimate experience than its well-known neighbor. Part of a town-owned park and campground, it includes picnic areas, playing fields, and a short trail that leads to one of the area's best-kept secrets: Eagle Cliff Falls.

This 40-foot cascade is tucked into a narrow, mossy gorge. The trail—about a quarter mile—follows a shallow creek bed beneath towering cliffs, then leads to a metal staircase clinging to the gorge wall before delivering you to the base of the falls. Water plunges into a rocky basin surrounded by a natural amphitheater, where mist and sunlight create a dramatic setting. Havana Glen is a favorite among photographers, hikers, and families seeking a scenic, moderately challenging walk in a peaceful setting.

INSIDER TIP: A small cash-only entrance fee applies during the operating season (typically May–October). Bring water shoes if you want to wade in the creek.

The Eternal Flame Trail

6746 Chestnut Ridge Road, Orchard Park

Nestled within Chestnut Ridge Park in Orchard Park near Buffalo, the Eternal Flame Trail leads to one of New York's most remarkable natural wonders: a small flame burning behind a waterfall. Sustained by a natural gas seep and sheltered in a shale alcove, it's one of only a few places on Earth where fire and water coexist.

The hike starts from a large parking lot off Route 277 and descends a 135-step wooden staircase into a steep, shaded ravine. From there, a creekside path winds about 0.6 miles upstream toward the falls. There is no formal trail in the gorge—expect muddy banks, slippery rocks, and shallow water crossings. At the end, a 35-foot waterfall cascades over layered rock, and behind it, a flickering flame illuminates a rocky alcove. It's a short but challenging hike with a significant reward, combining geology, curiosity, and a hint of mystery.

INSIDER TIP: Bring a lighter in case the flame is out upon arrival. You'll be the hero to all who didn't know this tip!

Grimes Glen

Vine Street, Naples

Grimes Glen is one of the Finger Lakes Region's most immersive waterfall hikes. Just a short walk from downtown Naples, this scenic gorge invites you to step directly into the creek and follow the water upstream through a narrow canyon. The trail begins at the end of Vine Street, where a footbridge and a dirt path lead from a small parking lot to the creek bed. From there, it's a wet hike—wading over smooth, slippery stones through ankle-deep pools. There's no dry route; water shoes and a walking stick are essential.

About half a mile in, you'll reach the first 60-foot waterfall, a wide cascade pouring into a rocky basin. A second, more secluded 60-foot waterfall waits farther upstream, framed by dramatic cliffs. The complete round trip is under a mile, best enjoyed at a slow pace with time to explore.

INSIDER TIP: Polarized sunglasses help you see your footing on a sunny afternoon, and a dry pouch for your phone and keys is a must. Pack a towel and a change of clothes—you'll likely get wet.

Holley Canal Falls

1 Holley Falls Park Road, Holley

One of the most picturesque hidden gems along the Erie Canal, Holley Canal Falls is fed by overflow from the canal itself, making it one of the few waterfalls in New York powered by a man-made waterway. It spills steadily over a red Medina sandstone ledge into Sandy Creek, right in the heart of the village. Park at the end of Frisbee Terrace to view the falls from your car. Walk over the culvert to reach the base or cross the footbridge to follow the trail to the top. Continue upstream to see where it flows from the canal.

Paved and gravel trails lead through the small park to multiple viewpoints. Interpretive signs along the loop highlight the Erie Canal's role in Holley's development, and the nearby Holley Depot Museum—open Sundays or by appointment—adds historical context to the area's transportation legacy.

INSIDER TIP: In the heat of summer, when many waterfalls slow to a trickle, this one often maintains a reliable flow thanks to consistent canal runoff.

Stony Brook

10820 Route 36 South, Dansville

Stony Brook State Park in Dansville is a classic Finger Lakes gorge park. The Gorge Trail is a 3/4-mile path that follows Stony Brook through a narrow shale and sandstone canyon. Along the way, you'll cross stone bridges, climb stairways, and pause beside waterfalls framed by mossy cliffs. The terrain isn't steep, but it can be uneven and wet in places. Above the gorge, the East and West Rim Trails offer a different perspective, winding through the forest and meadow landscape with occasional views into the canyon.

In summer, the park's refreshing, natural stream-fed swimming pool adds a nostalgic highlight. The lifeguards may close the pool due to inclement weather at any time, so call ahead if swimming is a crucial part of your visit. Please be advised that the park discourages wading in the gorge and will issue fines to those who do so.

INSIDER TIP: Most visitors hike the Gorge Trail in and out to appreciate a different perspective each way.

Akron Falls

44 Parkview Drive, Akron

Akron Falls Park is a 284-acre Erie County Park that feels both accessible and remote. Its centerpiece is a 40-foot waterfall on Murder Creek, cascading into a shaded ravine surrounded by mossy rocks and tall trees. From a lot near the rock garden, visitors can take a zigzagging, paved trail down toward the creek and choose to head right to the overlook or left toward the forest floor. Or start your hike from the main parking lot near the dam for a leisurely walk along the creek.

Those who explore beyond the waterfall will find trails winding amidst the creek's moss-covered boulders under a thick tree canopy, creating a tunnel of lush green hues in summer. In winter, the frozen falls create a towering sculpture of ice. Loved by locals but rarely crowded, the park is ideal for a peaceful walk, casual photography, or a quiet family outing.

INSIDER TIP: For quick access to the waterfall, park in the lot off Skyline Drive near the rock garden and follow the paved path toward the creek.

Rock City Park

505 Rock City Road, Olean

Perched high above a valley, Rock City Park in Olean is a 23-acre landscape of towering boulders, narrow crevices, and panoramic views. It's home to one of the world's most significant exposures of quartz conglomerate, formed over 300 million years ago by ancient rivers flowing across what is now western New York.

A half-mile loop trail winds through named formations like Sentinel Rock, the Three Sisters, and Balancing Rock, beginning with a scenic cliff-top view and descending a steep stairway into shaded stone corridors. Moss, lichen, and filtered light give the trail a peaceful, otherworldly feel. In the late 1800s, the park was a major attraction, complete with a hotel and dance pavilion. Some visitors' names, carved into the stone over a century ago, can still be seen. Please leave no such evidence of your visit.

INSIDER TIP: To appreciate the park without the steep descent, take the short path behind the gift shop to Signal Rock, where an overlook offers stunning views. Inside the museum, you can also watch a video tour—perfect for those who prefer to stay above the gorge.

Medina Falls

325 East Center Street, Medina

Just steps from downtown, Medina Falls is a 40-foot cascade hiding in plain sight. Its unique source sets it apart: Oak Orchard Creek flows under the Erie Canal aqueduct through a culvert before reemerging, plunging over a red Medina sandstone ledge as a 150-foot curtain into a shaded gorge. Although not visible from the road, the falls are easily reached with a short walk along the Erie Canalway Trail. As you approach, the sound of rushing water grows louder, revealing a view of the falls from the canal towpath. With the quiet canal on one side and the roar of the falls on the other, it's a memorable and peaceful place to pause.

Park in the lot off Laurel Street, near the Horan Road bridge, and then walk west along the towpath. From State Street Park, see where Oak Orchard enters the culvert.

INSIDER TIP: Put in a kayak at Glenwood Lake and paddle upstream to view the falls from below.

Fillmore Glen

1686 State Route 38, Moravia

Just outside the village of Moravia at the southern end of Skaneateles Lake, Fillmore Glen State Park offers a quieter gorge experience with as much beauty as its more famous Finger Lakes neighbors. Named for President Millard Fillmore, who was born nearby, the park features a narrow gorge, five waterfalls, and peaceful woodland trails. Near the entrance, a replica of Fillmore's childhood log cabin gives visitors a glimpse of the modest home where the future president spent his early years, adding a historical layer to the natural beauty.

The Gorge Trail follows Dry Creek through a shaded canyon of cliffs, mossy ledges, and stone staircases. The shaded gorge remains refreshingly comfortable even on the hottest summer days, as the dense forest canopy forms a cool green tunnel.

INSIDER TIP: As you hike past the natural stream-fed swimming area, cross the footbridge for a rewarding detour from the main gorge trail to discover the impressive 56-foot Cow Shed Falls, the lowest of Dry Creek's notable cascades.

Moss Lake Preserve

8461 Sand Hill Road, Caneadea

Born of ice and time, Moss Lake formed when a block of glacial ice melted fifteen thousand years ago, leaving a steep-sided basin that slowly developed a floating mat of sphagnum moss. This living sponge creates ideal conditions for orchids, carnivorous plants, and other bog specialists, earning the site designation as a National Natural Landmark in 1973. Managed by The Nature Conservancy, Moss Lake is among the best-preserved kettle bogs in New York—and a peaceful retreat for nature lovers.

A quiet one-mile loop trail circles the bog, with a 0.3-mile wheelchair-accessible approach and a 150-foot boardwalk that seems to hover over the moss. Dragonflies, frogs, and migrating birds frequent the area, while the bowl and doily spider spins its intricate web just inches from the walkway. Every step stays on planks, a reminder that the ground below is floating and alive.

INSIDER TIP: Visit in early fall for fiery reflections and wildlife activity. But tread gently—stay on the trail and don't feed the fish.

Hemlock Lake Park

7412 Rix Hill Road, Hemlock

Hemlock Lake Park provides one of the quietest and most unspoiled Finger Lakes experiences. As part of Rochester's protected water supply, Hemlock has avoided the development and tourism common at other lakes. There are no marinas, restaurants, or commercial attractions—just still water, wooded slopes, and a deep sense of calm.

At the lake's northern end, the park offers a shaded picnic area, a small playground, and a scenic gazebo. Because the state limits development, the lake feels surprisingly wild. Hemlock-Canadice State Forest rises sharply from the shore, and the water is so clear you can often see straight to the bottom.

INSIDER TIP: Hemlock Lake offers excellent conditions for stargazing and astrophotography on clear nights. The low level of light pollution provides clearer views of stars, planets, meteor showers, and the Milky Way.

Lamberton Conservatory

180 Reservoir Avenue, Rochester

Located in Highland Park, the Lamberton Conservatory is a bright, glass-enclosed greenhouse that offers warmth, color, and calm year-round. Stepping inside, the outside world fades away. Tropical air, the sound of running water, and layered greenery slow the pace almost immediately.

The conservatory is organized into distinct environments. Humid rooms feature palms, banana trees, and plants draped with Spanish moss, while the desert house offers dry air and bright light, filled with cacti and other arid-climate species. Turtles rest near ponds, and button quail and tortoises move quietly through the plantings.

In winter, especially, Lamberton feels like a small but meaningful escape—filled with growth, color, and light when much of the landscape outside is dormant.

INSIDER TIP: During the Holiday Show, the conservatory opens on Friday and Sunday evenings from December through early January—a rare chance to experience the space after dark, when festive lights glow against the glass and greenery.

The Sunken Garden

5 Castle Park, Rochester

Tucked behind Warner Castle in Highland Park near Mount Hope Cemetery, the Sunken Garden is one of Rochester's most enchanting under-the-radar spaces. Designed in 1930 by landscape architect Alling DeForest—best known for the gardens at the George Eastman Museum—this walled garden feels like a hidden oasis. Regardless of the season, the space holds a quiet stillness.

Despite its charm, the garden is often overlooked by casual park visitors, making it ideal for calm reflection. Warner Castle—home to the Landmark Society of Western New York—adds historical depth to the experience, even though the building itself is closed to the public.

INSIDER TIP: Try to visit on a weekday or earlier in the day. The Sunken Garden is a popular setting for professional photography and may be reserved for private sessions, which can limit access during scheduled shoots.

Durand Eastman Park Arboretum

Pine Valley Road, Rochester

The Durand Eastman Park Arboretum began in 1907, when Dr. Henry Durand and George Eastman deeded 484 acres of lakeside land to the city of Rochester for a public park. In 1908, the city's botanist, Bernard H. Slavin, set about turning the sandy bluffs into a living tree atlas, raising seedlings on-site and importing stock from Highland Park and Harvard's Arnold Arboretum.

Today, the collection extends east from Durand Lake to Culver Road. A mile-long drive follows Zoo and Pine Valley Roads, while a paved, 0.4-mile, car-free lane between Log Cabin and Zoo Roads skirts kettle ponds, where benches and plant labels make the stroll enjoyable for both casual walkers and botanists. Explore the diverse collections from Rose Valley to Pine Valley, which feature magnolia, cherry, oak, maple, tulip poplar, witch hazel, and dogwood, all set against the backdrop of a varied evergreen pinetum.

INSIDER TIP: In early November, dozens of katsura trees in Katsura Glen—located on Zoo Road near Durand Lake and Lake Shore Boulevard—drop golden, heart-shaped leaves and scent the air like cotton candy.

Griffis Sculpture Park

6902 Mill Valley Road, East Otto

Griffis Sculpture Park is where art and nature collide across 450 acres of rolling hills, wooded trails, and open meadows in East Otto. It's one of the oldest and largest sculpture parks in the country, yet it still feels like a hidden discovery. More than 250 large-scale sculptures, crafted from steel, wood, and stone, are scattered throughout the landscape. Some rise boldly in fields, while others hide in the trees. You might find yourself climbing a massive spider, posing beside whimsical humanoid figures, or peering through abstract forms that frame the landscape in unexpected ways.

The park is divided into two areas: Rohr Hill, featuring roadside sculptures, and Mill Valley, where the trails range from easy to moderately challenging, offering plenty of space to explore and interact with the art.

INSIDER TIP: Use cash or Venmo for the modest admission and wear sturdy shoes. Some trails can be extremely muddy after rainfall, and you'll want to explore them all.

Webster Arboretum

1700 Schlegel Road, Webster

The 32-acre Webster Arboretum is nestled within Kent Park, a larger community space that features ballfields and open recreation areas. In contrast, the arboretum offers a peaceful retreat of curated gardens, walking paths, and shaded corners—lovingly maintained by volunteers and quietly cherished by those who visit. Themed areas include a conifer collection, antique rose garden, daylily and dahlia beds, and a thoughtfully arranged herb garden. Flat gravel paths wind through the grounds, leading to a reflective pond, wooden bridges, gazebos, and benches perfect for lingering.

A lesser-known event is when, during Webster's 1990 sesquicentennial celebration, community members buried a time capsule beneath a crabapple tree near the park's entrance. They plan to unearth it in 2039, revealing a small, hidden marker of the town's history.

INSIDER TIP: Visit in July to see the daylilies at their peak. With more than 200 cultivars in the collection, bloom times vary, so each visit reveals a new wave of color and form.

Delaware Park Japanese Garden

1 Museum Court, Buffalo

While most visitors to Buffalo's Delaware Park spend their time around scenic Hoyt Lake, crossing the Scajaquada Expressway leads to a quieter gem: the Japanese Garden behind the Buffalo History Museum.

Created in partnership with Buffalo's sister city of Kanazawa, Japan, this peaceful retreat features arched bridges, stone lanterns, and more than 1,000 plantings. Three small islands float on Mirror Lake, whose still waters reflect the garden's grace and balance. Originally connected to the mainland by bridges, these islands are now decorative only, enhancing the tranquil scenery. In spring, cherry blossoms bloom during the annual festival. Come fall, Japanese maples burst into vibrant color.

INSIDER TIP: Park at the Buffalo History Museum and take time to explore inside—admission is affordable, and exhibits highlight Western New York's rich history. From the museum's back lawn, stroll down to the Japanese Garden, where you can spot the seated bronze statue of Abraham Lincoln overlooking the serene landscape.

Sycamore Hill Gardens

2130 Old Seneca Turnpike, Marcellus

Tucked into the rolling hills outside Marcellus, Sycamore Hill Gardens feels like a secret world—carefully shaped by imagination, artistry, and a deep love for the land. This privately owned garden estate spans over 30 acres and invites visitors to explore a rich tapestry of design, where formal structure meets whimsical beauty.

Wander among Asian and European sculptures, tranquil koi ponds, and carefully crafted stonework. A formal garden bursts with color and texture throughout the growing season, while expansive lawns offer panoramic views of the surrounding countryside. One of the most extraordinary features is the hedge maze that invites a sense of play. Every path and planting reflects the vision of the Hanford family, who have spent decades traveling and cultivating this living, evolving masterpiece.

INSIDER TIP: Self-guided visits are available by reservation only, seven days a week. Admission is per vehicle (up to eight people), so feel free to bring friends to explore together.

Ellwanger Garden

625 Mt. Hope Avenue, Rochester

Ellwanger Garden is a historic half-acre garden in Rochester on Mt. Hope Avenue, established in 1867 by George Ellwanger, a prominent 19th-century horticulturist. In the 1920s and '30s, landscape architect Fletcher Steele was commissioned to enhance the garden's design, incorporating elements that reflected his distinctive style.

Today, the garden is maintained by the Landmark Society of Western New York and features a diverse collection of perennials, trees, and shrubs, including heritage lilacs, peonies, and irises. Boxwood-lined pathways and the sense of enclosure achieved by the tall trees that line the garden's perimeter charm visitors even in the absence of riotous color. Ellwanger Garden is open to the public on weekends during the Lilac Festival in May and Peony Weekend in June.

INSIDER TIP: There is no on-site parking at Ellwanger Garden. Visitors should park at the University of Rochester's Health and Safety Building, located at 685 Mt. Hope Avenue, accessible via McLean Street. This parking area is adjacent to the garden.

Linwood Gardens

1912 York Road West, Linwood

Nestled into the countryside between Geneseo and Pavilion, Linwood Gardens is a private estate that opens for just a few weekends each spring to showcase one of the region's most breathtaking displays: its world-class collection of blooming tree peonies. The Tree Peony Festival of Flowers, held from late May through early June, transforms the garden into a living canvas of color, fragrance, and form.

From the 1930s to the 1980s, Linwood was a center for American tree peony hybridization, thanks to the work of William H. Gratwick III and artist-horticulturist Nassos Daphnis, whose cultivars are still admired worldwide. The garden's Arts and Crafts–inspired design features stone walls, terraced beds, and long views over the Genesee Valley. Visitors can wander at their own pace or join a guided tour of the grounds and historic home, often led by descendants of the Gratwick family.

INSIDER TIP: Reservations are required during festival weekends and fill up quickly. Arrive early for the softest light, fewer crowds, and stunning photo opportunities.

George Eastman Estate Gardens

900 East Avenue, Rochester

Easily overlooked by passersby, the estate gardens at the George Eastman Museum in Rochester offer a refined burst of color and calm in the heart of the city. Shaded pathways, stone features, and curated plantings invite quiet reflection or a peaceful pause. While admission is required to explore the formal Italianate Terrace Garden and Library Garden—both designed by landscape architect Alling Stephen DeForest—the West Garden and Rock Garden are free and open to the public.

The Rock Garden, also designed by DeForest, offers a more informal setting beneath magnificent ginkgo trees and a grape arbor. The West Garden, conceived by architect Claude Bragdon in 1917, draws inspiration from English walled gardens, featuring symmetrical plantings and a stone loggia. At its western edge, the loggia shelters a bronze lion's head fountain set into a mosaic-tiled wall.

INSIDER TIP: Visit in mid-May to catch the purple and white wisteria at its peak, when the West Garden becomes one of the most photogenic spots in the city.

Sonnenberg Gardens

151 Charlotte Street, Canandaigua

A short walk from downtown Canandaigua, Sonnenberg Gardens feels like stepping into another era. This 50-acre estate combines the grandeur of a Gilded Age mansion with the quiet wonder of nine formal and naturalistic gardens—each with its own style, rhythm, and season of beauty.

The Italian Garden is a symmetrical showpiece, its fountains and stonework evoking classical grandeur. The Japanese Garden, complete with a torii gate, tea house, and koi pond, exudes serenity. For a more secluded experience, the Rock Garden offers winding paths through alpine plantings and quiet pools. Visitors can also explore the greenhouse complex, designed by the renowned Lord & Burnham company, one of the last surviving examples of its kind in the country.

INSIDER TIP: After exploring the gardens, visit the Finger Lakes Wine Center, located in the estate's historic Bay House. The tasting room features a rotating selection of local wines, with its centerpiece being a 1911 Tiffany-style stained-glass window crafted by Rochester's Pike Stained Glass Studio.

Sara's Garden Center

389 East Avenue, Brockport

At first glance, Sara's Garden Center in Brockport looks like a well-stocked, well-loved local nursery—overflowing with seasonal plants, colorful containers, and cheerful staff ready to help. But follow the paths behind the greenhouses, and you'll discover something much more unexpected: a sprawling landscaped garden where artistry and horticulture meet in spectacular fashion.

Stone walls twist and rise into arches, framing garden rooms with reflective ponds, shaded seating, and vibrant plantings. A backdrop of towering American arborvitae forms a natural green wall, adding structure and seclusion while enhancing the sense of discovery. Carefully manicured beds brim with seasonal color, and sculptural elements work together to create the feeling of a living exhibit.

INSIDER TIP: Don't miss the moon gate—a circular stone arch that perfectly frames the lush landscape beyond. When viewed from the right angle, it creates a near-perfect reflection in the adjacent pool—a postcard-worthy vision of tranquility.

Ganondagan

7000 County Road 41, Victor

Perched atop Boughton Hill in Victor, Ganondagan is the only New York State Historic Site devoted to Native American heritage. In the 1600s, more than 150 bark longhouses sheltered some 4,500 Hodinöhsö:ni' residents, forming a diplomatic and agricultural hub until French forces destroyed it during the 1687 Beaver Wars. Today, the Seneca Art & Culture Center anchors the 569-acre landscape with exhibits, films, and a replica longhouse.

Beyond the building, marked trails wind through fields, hardwood forest, and sacred earthworks. Adjacent hillside plots host the Iroquois White Corn Project, where heirloom Tuscarora White kernels are husked, roasted, and stone-ground into flour that funds food-sovereignty initiatives and winter cornbread workshops.

INSIDER TIP: Visit in late July during the Indigenous Music and Arts Festival, when the site comes alive with storytelling, drumming, dancing, traditional food, and celebration. Centered on Hodinöhsö:ni' culture yet welcoming Indigenous voices from around the world, the festival showcases a talented new lineup each year.

The Clock of Nations

Tower280, 280 Broad Street, Rochester

Once the centerpiece of Midtown Plaza, the Clock of Nations now resides in the lobby of Tower280, just steps from where it first captivated Rochesterians in the 1960s. Following the closure of Midtown Plaza, the clock spent a few years on display at the Greater Rochester International Airport before being stored away. Its preservation and restoration were made possible by Ken Glazer of Buckingham Properties, whose efforts brought this beloved timepiece back to life.

Daily, from 7 a.m. to 7 p.m., 12 cultural vignettes rotate continuously to music, transforming the lobby into a living exhibit of international artistry. Each animated capsule in this whimsical, midcentury mechanical clock represents a nation significant to Rochester's cultural landscape in the 1960s, reflecting the city's long-standing diversity.

INSIDER TIP: After your visit, cross over to Mercantile on Main to see the restored Sibley clock, another midtown Rochester artifact. Together, they form a nostalgic presence that celebrates Rochester—and how it continues to tick forward.

Olcott Beach

Ontario Street, Olcott

Olcott Beach is one of Western New York's most nostalgic waterfront escapes—a vintage resort town nestled along the south shore of Lake Ontario that still pulses with the spirit of summers past. It's a place where classic amusements, cheerful shops, and breezy lake views converge in the kind of simple magic that appeals to all.

At the heart of the experience is Olcott Beach Carousel Park, a pint-sized amusement park designed especially for children under 52" tall. The restored 1920s rides cost just a quarter. Only steps away, the Lakeview Village Shoppes line the wooden boardwalk in a row of pastel-painted cottages. These seasonal shops sell handmade gifts, vintage finds, jewelry, and ice cream, made even sweeter by the sights and sounds of Lake Ontario.

INSIDER TIP: The carousel park is open from noon to 6 p.m. Saturday and Sunday in June, and Friday through Sunday from July through Labor Day.

Lily Dale Assembly

5 Melrose Park, Lily Dale

Lily Dale Assembly is one of the world's oldest and most respected spiritualist communities. Nestled along the quiet shores of Cassadaga Lake, this peaceful, gated village has welcomed the spiritually curious since 1879. Lily Dale opens for a summer season of lectures, healing circles, workshops, and mediumship demonstrations. More than 50 registered mediums live and practice here. Visitors are invited to attend gatherings at the Forest Temple, receive healing in the Healing Temple, or sit in quiet awe at Inspiration Stump.

The village itself is steeped in Victorian charm, with colorful cottages, abundant gardens, spiritual bookstores, and woodland trails that encourage reflection. Guests are free to participate as much—or as little—as they like.

INSIDER TIP: If you're hoping for a private reading, make a reservation online or arrive early to sign up with a medium. Midweek visits are quieter and offer more opportunities for stillness and connection.

The Old Erie Canal Heritage Park

1575 Rooker Drive, Port Byron

Located along a quieter stretch of the Erie Canalway Trail, Old Erie Canal Heritage Park in Port Byron offers a vivid glimpse into 19th-century canal life. At its heart stand the preserved Enlarged Erie Canal Lock 52 and restored 1853 Erie House, once a tavern and boarding house for weary canal travelers.

The grounds include a mule barn, working models, and interpretive signage that bring to life the day-to-day experience of canal travel during the height of New York's canal era. The park is also now the permanent home of the canal schooner *Lois McClure*. This full-scale replica cargo vessel anchors the site's maritime interpretation, deepening visitors' understanding of canal commerce and New York's working waterfront history.

INSIDER TIP: This is the only park in the United States with direct access from a major thruway. From May to October, travelers heading eastbound on I-90 can exit directly into the park after the Port Byron service plaza. Local visitors can use Rooker Drive, off NY-31, for back-road access.

ARTISANworks

565 Blossom Road, Rochester

ARTISANworks is a creative wonderland in Rochester where art bursts off the walls, dangles from the ceiling, and transforms every inch into a curated spectacle. Housed in a sprawling 40,000-square-foot former warehouse, it's not just a gallery—it's an out-of-body experience.

The 500,000+ piece collection features original works by world-renowned artists such as Picasso, Warhol, Miro, and Dali, alongside Wendelle Castle, Ramon Santiago, and other local artists. But what sets ARTISANworks apart is its playful, theatrical spirit: rooms dedicated to Marilyn Monroe and Kodak memorabilia, a life-sized giraffe, and a larger-than-life wooden pencil sharpener, as well as a Frank Lloyd Wright–inspired dining room adjacent to a retro rec room.

INSIDER TIP: Visitors are encouraged to explore freely—you might feel overwhelmed and get turned around, but you will never be completely lost. On Saturday and Sunday, guided tours provide access to a vintage car gallery and themed event spaces, transporting you from Mel's Diner to Casablanca.

The Cobblestone Museum

14393 Ridge Road West, Albion

Along historic Route 104, the Cobblestone Museum in Childs provides a fascinating glimpse into a uniquely regional architectural style. Western New York boasts the largest concentration of cobblestone buildings in the United States, with over 800 recorded in its database, 90% of which are located within a 75-mile radius of Rochester. This museum complex preserves some of the most remarkable examples.

At the center of the site is a trio of original 19th-century structures: a cobblestone church (the oldest in North America), a parsonage, and a district schoolhouse. Built with thousands of hand-laid glacial stones collected from nearby Lake Ontario, these buildings are a testament to the craftsmanship and ingenuity of early settlers. The grounds include a blacksmith shop, print shop, farmhouse, and other relocated buildings that form a condensed 19th-century village.

INSIDER TIP: Plan your visit during one of the museum's seasonal events or heritage days to see live demonstrations by artisans.

Abbey of the Genesee

3258 River Road, Piffard

Home to a community of Trappist monks since 1951, the Abbey of the Genesee in Piffard is best known for its Monks' Bread. While the bakery draws many first-time visitors, the real gift of the abbey is its quiet invitation to slow down and savor the moment. Guests are welcome to enter the chapel quietly. Low light filters into the chapel through colorful faceted stained-glass windows built into a stone wall, providing a soothing backdrop for prayer, reflection, or a moment of silence. Gregorian chants can be heard as part of the daily liturgy.

Though photography is prohibited inside the chapel and in monastic areas, visitors are free to explore the surrounding grounds, admire the abbey's simple architecture, or walk the nearby woodland trails. The monks live by the Rule of St. Benedict, emphasizing prayer, work, and community—a rhythm that shapes every aspect of abbey life.

INSIDER TIP: Visitors are welcome to attend public services at the abbey. The daily liturgical schedule is available online and ranges from 3:30 a.m. Vigils to 7:30 p.m. Compline.

Wat Pa Lao Buddhadham

135 Martin Road, West Henrietta

Tucked into a quiet corner of West Henrietta, Wat Pa Lao Buddhadham feels worlds away. Although it is an active place of worship, respectful visitors are welcome to wander the outdoor grounds and take photos any day between 7 a.m. and 5 p.m. At its heart rises the majestic Ordination Hall (Sim), whose steeply tiered red roof rises over golden diamond-patterned walls that gleam in the sun. Bronze lions flank the entry to the grounds, while brightly painted zodiac-animal statues watch over the Sim from each corner, reflecting the Lao community's deep cultural roots.

A broad staircase descends from the Sim to the focal point of a tranquil Zen garden: a beautiful rectangular reflecting pool ringed with pink lotus sculptures and guarded by Naga balustrades.

INSIDER TIP: Visit during the Summer Kickoff Food Festival in early June to enjoy the grounds while savoring delicious Lao and Thai cuisine and live music. This is the only event of the year where guests are invited inside the Sim to view and photograph the mural-lined sanctuary and speak with one of the monks.

Garrett Memorial Chapel

5251 Skyline Drive, Keuka Park

Perched high above Keuka Lake on Bluff Point in Jerusalem, Garrett Memorial Chapel is one of the Finger Lakes' most serene and striking landmarks. Built in 1931 by the Garrett family in memory of their son Charles, who died young, this Gothic-style stone chapel offers a sacred space for reflection with unforgettable views. The chapel's interior features leaded-glass windows and intricate woodwork. A warm plaster vault and stone ribs curve overhead, creating an intimate, amber-lit space. Surrounding the building are scenic overlooks, woodland paths, and simple benches where visitors can pause and soak in the sweeping lake vista.

Parking is limited—a small driveway fits just a few cars. If spots are full, park along the upper road and walk the switchback trail down to the chapel. Use care when turning around, as the terrain can be uneven and roadside ditches are hard to see.

INSIDER TIP: Visit on a Tuesday or Thursday in summer (June–September) to step inside the chapel's ornate interior. For solitude, aim for a spring or late fall weekday.

Our Lady of Fatima Shrine

1023 Swann Road, Youngstown

Our Lady of Fatima Shrine in Lewiston offers a peaceful and unexpected experience, where spiritual architecture, landscaped gardens, and large-scale art converge in a space that feels both meditative and surreal. Set on 16 acres, the Roman Catholic shrine invites visitors to wander the Avenue of Saints, featuring 100+ life-size marble statues—all anchored by a towering dome with a 13-foot statue of Mary.

The circular basilica is both simple and striking. Inside, stained-glass windows light curved pews, and a glowing oculus above the altar draws the eye skyward. Central features include a bronze statue of the Three Children of Fatima and a heart-shaped Rosary Pool, outlined with 59 lights and concluding with a marble crucifix, which forms one of the largest outdoor rosaries in the world. Though a pilgrimage site, the shrine welcomes visitors of all backgrounds, offering beauty, stillness, and space to explore at your own pace.

INSIDER TIP: Climb the 63 steps to the top of the dome for sweeping views of the shrine grounds.

About the Author

Debi Bower is a photographer, travel writer, and web designer based in Rochester, New York. She is the creator of *Day Trips Around Rochester, New York*—a website and collection of books celebrating local exploration throughout the Finger Lakes and Western New York. Through photography and words, she invites readers to slow down, look closely, and rediscover the beauty of familiar places.

More Books by Debi Bower

Day Trips Around Rochester, New York
A guide to exploring destinations within two hours of Rochester and the Finger Lakes.

Hidden Places Around Rochester, New York
A Photographic Journey Through Western New York and the Finger Lakes

www.ingramcontent.com/pod-product-compliance
Lightning Source LLC
Chambersburg PA
CBHW050814160726

48004CB00002B/831